GRAPHIC DINOSAURS

ICHTHYOSAURUS

THE FISH LIZARD

ILLUSTRATED BY TERRY RILEY, ROB SHONE, JAMIE WEST

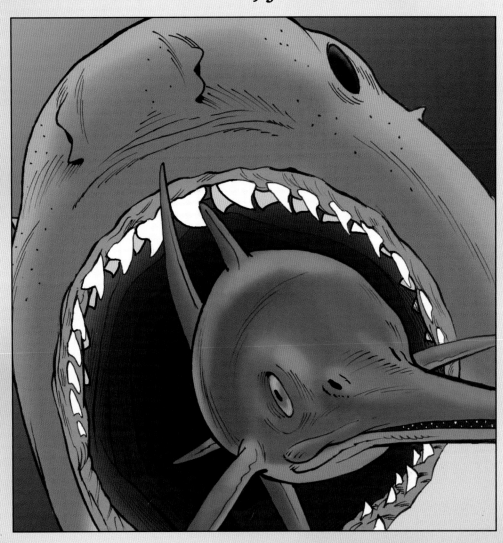

PowerKiDS
press.
New York

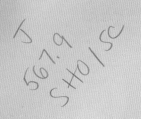

Published in 2012 by The Rosen Publishing Group, Inc.
29 East 21st Street, New York, NY 10010

Designed and produced by
David West Books

Designed and written by Rob Shone

Photographic credits: 5m, NOAA; 5b, NASA; 30m, Ballista; 30b, Steinsky

Library of Congress Cataloging-in-Publication Data
Shone, Rob.
Ichthyosaurus : the fish lizard / by Rob Shone.
p. cm. — (Graphic dinosaurs)
Includes index.
ISBN 978-1-4488-5206-2 (library binding) — ISBN 978-1-4488-5250-5 (pbk.) —
ISBN 978-1-4488-5251-2 (6-pack)
1. Ichthyosaurus—Juvenile literature. I. Title.
QE862.I2S56 2012
567.9'37—dc22
2010050974

Manufactured in China

CPSIA Compliance Information: Batch #DS1102PK:
For Further Information contact Rosen Publishing, New York, New York at 1-800-237-9932

CONTENTS

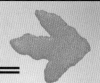

WHAT IS AN ICHTHYOSAURUS?

ICHTHYOSAURUS MEANS "FISH LIZARD."

◄ *Ichthyosaurus swam using just its powerful tail.*

◄ *The fin on Ichthyosaurus's back kept it upright in the water.*

◄ *Ichthyosaurus's skin was smooth, not scaly like that of many other reptiles.*

◄ *Ichthyosaurus could not bend its body. Its shape helped it move smoothly through the water.*

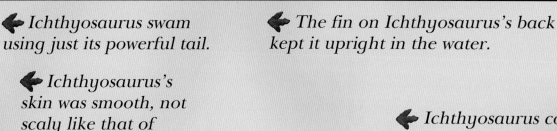

◄ *Ichthyosaurus's snout was long and thin and filled with sharp, cone-shaped teeth.*

◄ *Ichthyosaurus used its flippers to steer and to stop it from floating to the surface when it swam underwater.*

◄ *Its large eyes helped Ichthyosaurus find food in poor light. They were protected by bony rings.*

ICHTHYOSAURUS WAS A REPTILE THAT LIVED AROUND 200 TO 190 MILLION YEARS AGO, DURING THE JURASSIC PERIOD. FOSSILS OF ITS SKELETON HAVE BEEN FOUND IN EUROPE.

 Adult Ichthyosauruses measured up to 6.5 feet (2 m) long and weighed 200 pounds (90 kg).

A FAMILY HISTORY

Ichthyosaurus may have looked like a fish or a dolphin, but it was neither. It was a reptile that lived in the sea. At 6.5 feet (2 m) long, Ichthyosaurus was one of the smallest **ichthyosaurs**. The largest, Shonisaurus, grew to be up to 70 feet (21 m) in length. The first Ichthyosaurs appeared 250 million years ago, just before the dinosaurs. They looked very different when compared with Ichthyosaurus. Their bodies were long and thin, and they swam like eels. Ichthyosaurs finally became extinct 90 million years ago.

Ichthyosaurus's flippers kept it at the right depth when it swam underwater. The trim tanks on a submarine do the same job.

THE TETHYS OCEAN

Two hundred million years ago, when Ichthyosauruses lived, the world was very different. All the Earth's lands were bunched into two gigantic continents. To the east of these lands was Ichthyosaurus's home, the Tethys Ocean. Like today's tropical seas, the Tethys Ocean was warm. Much of it was shallow, and filled with a large variety of creatures.

Modern-day bluefin tuna (far left) are fish and not reptiles, but they have stiff, streamlined bodies and strong swimming tails like Ichthyosaurus. Although Ichthyosauruses looked like dolphins (left), they are not related.

PART ONE...

FRESH AIR

A CORAL REEF IN THE TETHYS OCEAN, 195 MILLION YEARS AGO.

A LARGE CREATURE APPROACHES. IT LOOKS LIKE A FISH, BUT IT IS NOT.

IT IS A FEMALE ICHTHYOSAURUS, A MARINE REPTILE. SHE HAS COME INTO THE SHALLOW LAGOON FROM THE OPEN OCEAN TO GIVE BIRTH.

SHE DOES NOT LAY EGGS ON LAND LIKE MOST OTHER REPTILES. HER YOUNG, CALLED PUPS, ARE BORN UNDERWATER, LIVE AND TAIL FIRST. ICHTHYOSAURUSES ARE AIR BREATHERS. IF THE PUPS WERE BORN HEADFIRST THEY MIGHT DROWN.

ONCE THEY ARE FREE OF THEIR MOTHER, THEY HAVE TO REACH THE SURFACE AS SOON AS THEY CAN.

THE LAGOON IS NOT DEEP, AND THE NEWBORN PUPS HAVE ONLY A SHORT JOURNEY TO ITS SURFACE.

THE BIRTH OF THE PUPS HAS ATTRACTED AN UNWANTED VISITOR. AN ATTENBOROSAURUS IS WATCHING THE ICHTHYOSAURUSES FROM THE SHADOWS OF THE REEF.

THE ATTENBOROSAURUS IS A PLESIOSAUR, A MEAT-EATING MARINE REPTILE. NEWBORN ICHTHYOSAURUS PUPS ARE A TASTY PART OF ITS DIET.

THERE IS ONE MORE ICHTHYOSAURUS TO BE BORN, THE FIFTH. THE PLESIOSAUR MOVES CLOSER.

THE LAST PUP IS BORN. HIS MOTHER SWIMS AWAY. SHE WILL HAVE NOTHING MORE TO DO WITH THE YOUNG ICHTHYOSAURUSES.

THE FIFTH PUP IS STRUGGLING TO GET TO THE SURFACE.

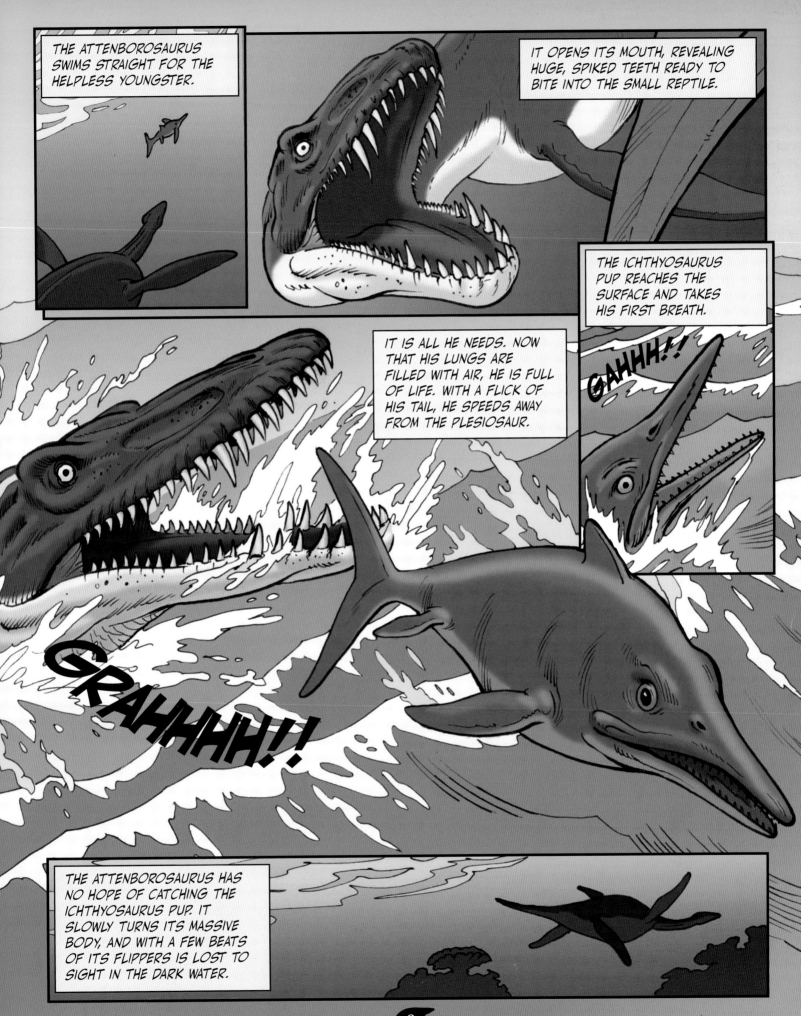

THE ATTENBOROSAURUS SWIMS STRAIGHT FOR THE HELPLESS YOUNGSTER.

IT OPENS ITS MOUTH, REVEALING HUGE, SPIKED TEETH READY TO BITE INTO THE SMALL REPTILE.

THE ICHTHYOSAURUS PUP REACHES THE SURFACE AND TAKES HIS FIRST BREATH.

IT IS ALL HE NEEDS. NOW THAT HIS LUNGS ARE FILLED WITH AIR, HE IS FULL OF LIFE. WITH A FLICK OF HIS TAIL, HE SPEEDS AWAY FROM THE PLESIOSAUR.

GAHH!!

GRAHHHH!!

THE ATTENBOROSAURUS HAS NO HOPE OF CATCHING THE ICHTHYOSAURUS PUP. IT SLOWLY TURNS ITS MASSIVE BODY, AND WITH A FEW BEATS OF ITS FLIPPERS IS LOST TO SIGHT IN THE DARK WATER.

PART TWO

THE SHELTER

A LEPIDOTES SWIMS OVER THE REEF. IT HAS SEEN A SNAIL.

THE FISH SHAPES ITS JAWS INTO A TUBE...

...AND SUCKS. THE SNAIL VANISHES INTO THE FISH'S MOUTH.

BERLOOP!!

THE FIFTH PUP WATCHES THE FISH.

HE HAS GROWN QUICKLY IN THE FEW WEEKS SINCE HIS BIRTH. THE REEF HAS BEEN HIS HOME. ITS MANY **NOOKS** AND **CRANNIES** HAVE SHELTERED HIM FROM DANGER. HE WILL STAY HERE IN THE SHALLOW WATER UNTIL HE IS BIG ENOUGH TO LIVE IN THE OPEN SEA.

THE LEPIDOTES CRUSHES THE SNAIL BETWEEN ROWS OF BROAD, FLAT TEETH. IT IGNORES THE PUP. THE FISH'S ARMORED SCALES ARE TOO THICK FOR THE ICHTHYOSAURUS TO DO IT ANY HARM.

SUDDENLY THE FISH SWIMS QUICKLY AWAY. THE PUP SENSES MOVEMENT NEARBY AND HIDES.

A POD OF TEMNODONTOSAURUSES PASSES OVER THE CORAL. THEY ARE ICHTHYOSAURS, LIKE THE PUP, BUT ARE MANY TIMES BIGGER. THESE GIANTS ARE ON THEIR WAY TO FEED IN THE DEEPEST AND DARKEST PART OF THE SEA. THEY USE THEIR HUGE EYES TO FIND THEIR PREY IN THE GLOOM.

TEMNODONTOSAURUSES FEED ON FISH AND SQUID, BUT THEY WILL ALSO EAT ICHTHYOSAURUSES. THE PUP WILL STAY HIDDEN UNTIL HE IS SURE THEY ARE GONE.

A SILVERY FLASH DARTS PAST THE PUP'S HIDING PLACE. THE MONSTER REPTILES HAVE DISTURBED A PHOLIDOPHORUS. THE PUP SETS OFF AFTER THE SLEEK FISH...

...AND CATCHES IT.

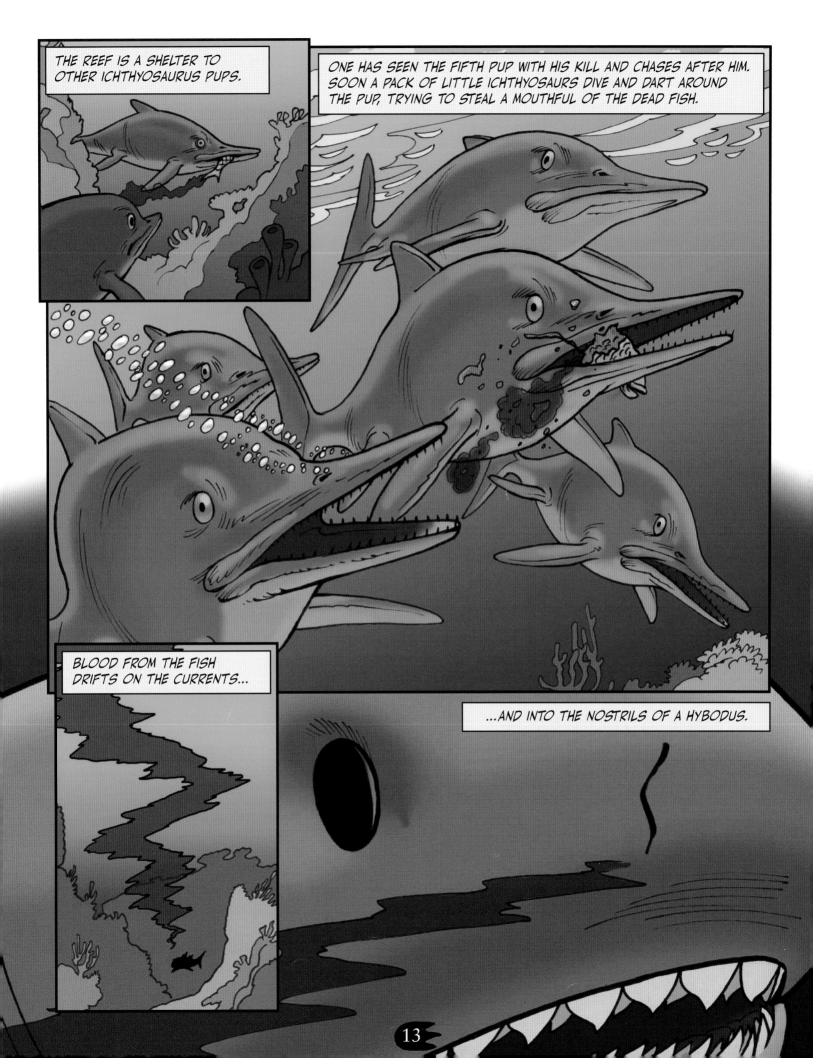

THE SCENT TRAIL LEADS THE SHARK TO THE SQUABBLING ICHTHYOSAURUSES.

THE PUPS HAVE STRAYED FROM THE SAFETY OF THE REEF. THE HYBODUS ATTACKS THEM.

THE ICHTHYOSAURUSES SWIM TO THE SURFACE OF THE WATER TO ESCAPE.

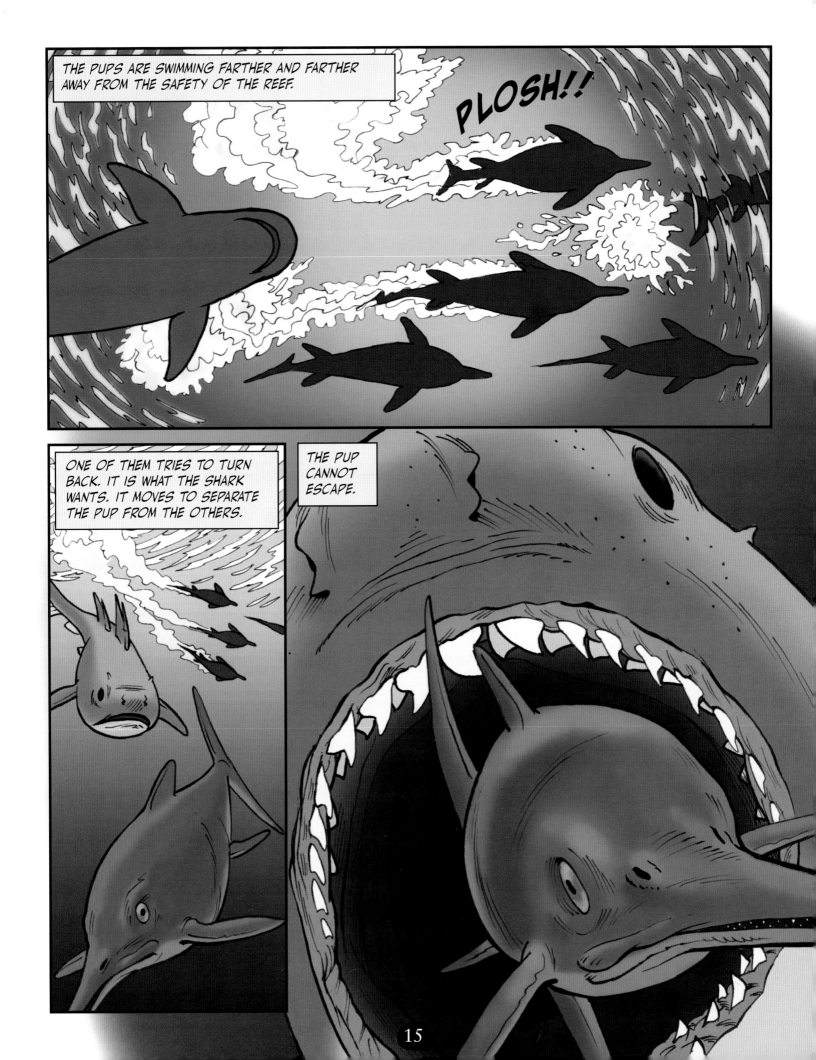

THE PUPS ARE SWIMMING FARTHER AND FARTHER AWAY FROM THE SAFETY OF THE REEF.

PLOSH!!

ONE OF THEM TRIES TO TURN BACK. IT IS WHAT THE SHARK WANTS. IT MOVES TO SEPARATE THE PUP FROM THE OTHERS.

THE PUP CANNOT ESCAPE.

BEFORE THE SHARK CAN KILL THE PUP, IT IS LIFTED FROM THE WATER, CAUGHT IN THE MASSIVE JAWS OF A TEMNODONTOSAURUS.

PERLOOOOSH!!

THE HUNTING TEMNODONTOSAURUSES HAVE RETURNED TO THE SURFACE TO BREATHE. THE HYBODUS HAS BECOME THEIR PREY.

NOT ALL THE ICHTHYOSAURUS PUPS ARE SAVED.

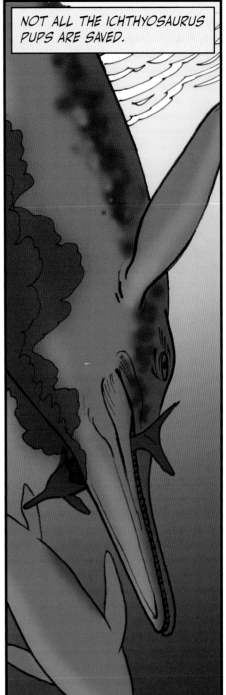

THE FIFTH PUP HAS REACHED THE REEF AND HAS FOUND A PLACE TO HIDE FROM SHARKS AND OTHER ICHTHYOSAURS. IT WILL BE SOME TIME BEFORE THE PUP IS BIG ENOUGH TO SWIM SAFELY IN THE OPEN OCEAN.

PART THREE... LIFE ON THE REEF

THE SUN RISES OVER THE TETHYS OCEAN AS A NEW DAY BEGINS. A MALE SARCOSAURUS IS WARMING HIMSELF IN THE MORNING SUNSHINE.

A PAIR OF SCELIDOSAURUSES ARE BROWSING NEARBY. THE SARCOSAURUS KNOWS THE PLANT EATERS ARE THERE, BUT HIS MUSCLES ARE STILL COLD FROM THE NIGHT. HE WILL HUNT THEM LATER.

DIMORPHODONS STIR ON THE CLIFFS ABOVE HIM.

THE FLYING REPTILES SWOOP DOWN FROM THEIR ROCKY ROOSTS AND HEAD OUT TO SEA IN SEARCH OF SMALL FISH TO EAT.

ARKK!!
ARKK!!
ARKK!!

ON THE SEASHORE A GROUP OF TELEOSAURUSES LIE BASKING IN THE SUNSHINE. THESE CROCODILES SPEND MOST OF THEIR LIVES AT SEA. AS THEY GET WARM, THEY SPLASH INTO THE WATER TO FEED.

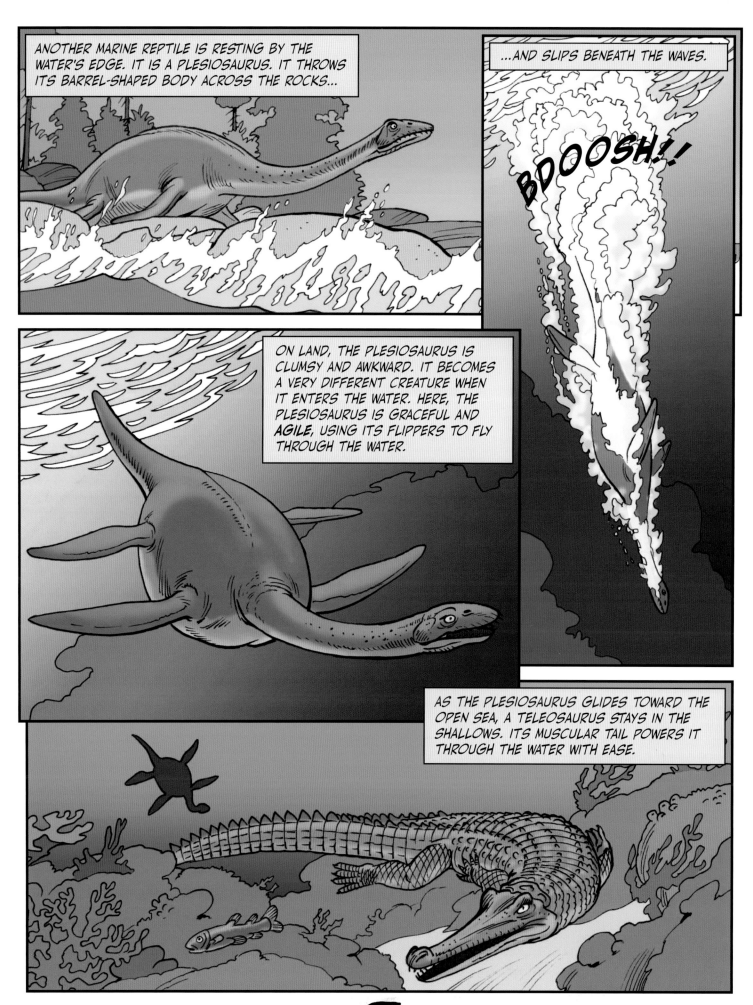

ANOTHER MARINE REPTILE IS RESTING BY THE WATER'S EDGE. IT IS A PLESIOSAURUS. IT THROWS ITS BARREL-SHAPED BODY ACROSS THE ROCKS...

...AND SLIPS BENEATH THE WAVES.

BDOOSH!!

ON LAND, THE PLESIOSAURUS IS CLUMSY AND AWKWARD. IT BECOMES A VERY DIFFERENT CREATURE WHEN IT ENTERS THE WATER. HERE, THE PLESIOSAURUS IS GRACEFUL AND *AGILE*, USING ITS FLIPPERS TO FLY THROUGH THE WATER.

AS THE PLESIOSAURUS GLIDES TOWARD THE OPEN SEA, A TELEOSAURUS STAYS IN THE SHALLOWS. ITS MUSCULAR TAIL POWERS IT THROUGH THE WATER WITH EASE.

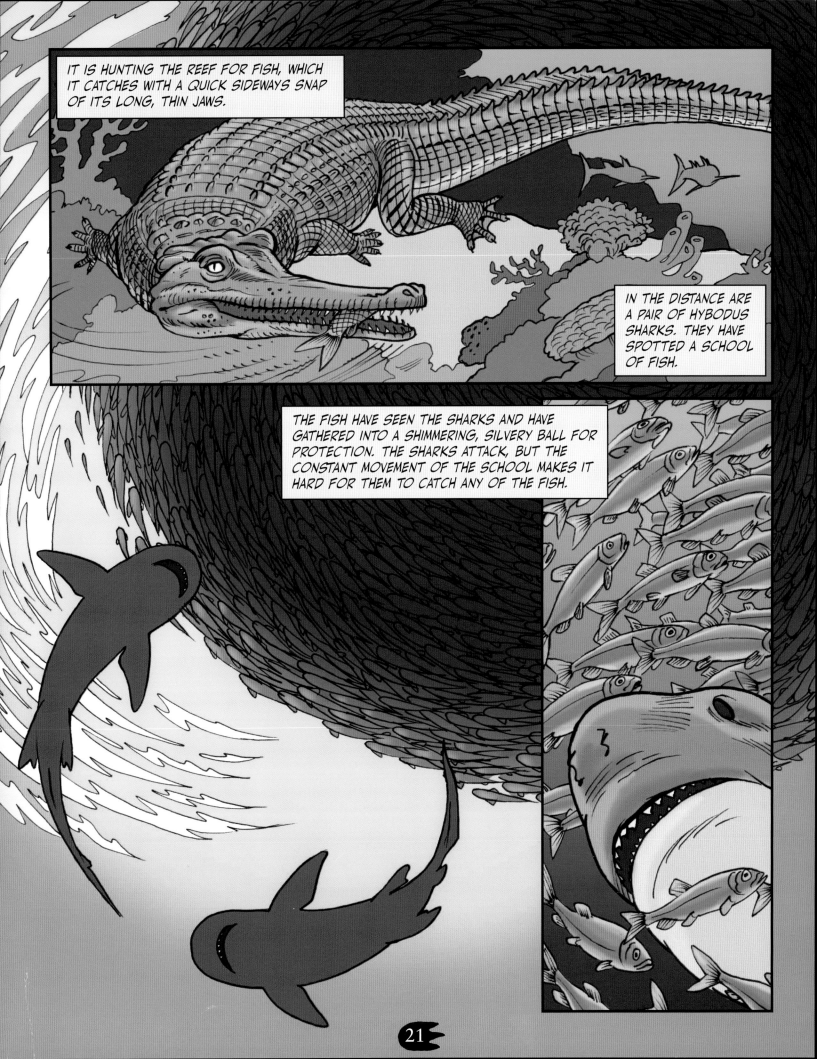

IT IS HUNTING THE REEF FOR FISH, WHICH IT CATCHES WITH A QUICK SIDEWAYS SNAP OF ITS LONG, THIN JAWS.

IN THE DISTANCE ARE A PAIR OF HYBODUS SHARKS. THEY HAVE SPOTTED A SCHOOL OF FISH.

THE FISH HAVE SEEN THE SHARKS AND HAVE GATHERED INTO A SHIMMERING, SILVERY BALL FOR PROTECTION. THE SHARKS ATTACK, BUT THE CONSTANT MOVEMENT OF THE SCHOOL MAKES IT HARD FOR THEM TO CATCH ANY OF THE FISH.

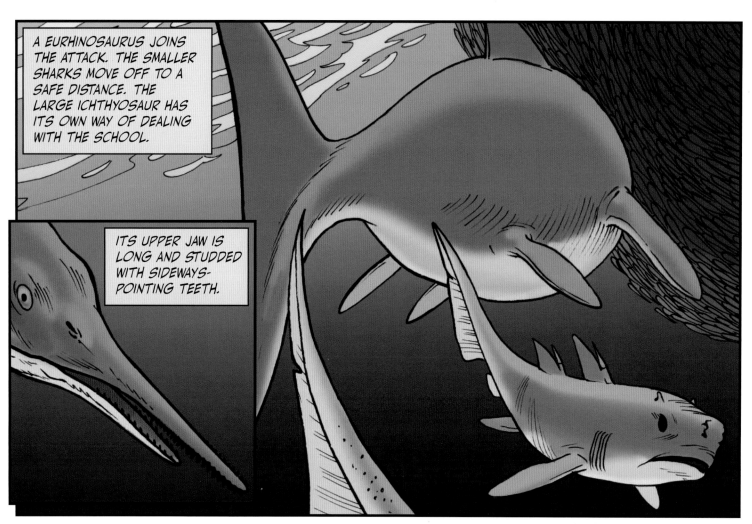

A EURHINOSAURUS JOINS THE ATTACK. THE SMALLER SHARKS MOVE OFF TO A SAFE DISTANCE. THE LARGE ICHTHYOSAUR HAS ITS OWN WAY OF DEALING WITH THE SCHOOL.

ITS UPPER JAW IS LONG AND STUDDED WITH SIDEWAYS-POINTING TEETH.

THE EURHINOSAURUS SWEEPS ITS SAWLIKE JAW THROUGH THE CROWD OF FISH, STUNNING SOME OF THEM.

THE DAZED FISH ARE GREEDILY EATEN BY THE REPTILE.

MEANWHILE, THE PLESIOSAURUS HAS SEEN ITS BREAKFAST...

...A GROUP OF AMMONITES, DISTANT RELATIVES OF SQUID AND OCTOPUS.

THE AMMONITE'S SHELL GIVES NO PROTECTION AGAINST THE PLESIOSAUR'S STRONG BITE.

LIKE SQUID, AMMONITES SQUIRT INK WHEN THEY ARE THREATENED.

THE SEA GROWS DARK FROM THE AMMONITES' INK, DARK ENOUGH TO HIDE A DEADLY RHOMALEOSAURUS.

THE RHOMALEOSAURUS IS A PLIOSAUR AND A FIERCE PREDATOR. IT WILL EAT ANYTHING IT CAN CATCH, INCLUDING PLESIOSAURUSES.

THE RHOMALEOSAURUS'S MASSIVE JAWS CLOSE AROUND THE SMALLER REPTILE, KILLING IT INSTANTLY.

THE PLIOSAUR SWALLOWS MOST OF ITS MEAL WHOLE. THE REST SINKS TO THE SEABED FOR THE SHARKS TO FINISH OFF.

A POD OF ICHTHYOSAURUSES IS FEEDING FARTHER FROM THE REEF. AMONG THEM IS THE FIFTH PUP. HE IS NOW ONE YEAR OLD AND AN ADULT.

THEY ARE HUNTING BELEMNITES, ANCIENT RELATIVES OF MODERN-DAY CUTTLEFISH AND SQUID. LIKE THE AMMONITES, BELEMNITES CAN SQUIRT BLACK INK INTO THE WATER TO CONFUSE PREDATORS.

THE SEA IS DEEPER HERE. LITTLE SUNLIGHT REACHES THESE DEPTHS, BUT THE ICHTHYOSAURUSES HAVE LARGE EYES TO SEEK OUT THEIR PREY.

UNLIKE AN AMMONITE'S, A BELEMNITE'S SHELL IS INSIDE ITS BODY. ICHTHYOSAURUSES CANNOT DIGEST THESE HARD PARTS, SO THEY VOMIT THEM UP ONTO THE SANDY OCEAN FLOOR.

THE ICHTHYOSAURUSES CAN STAY UNDERWATER FOR ONLY A SHORT TIME BEFORE THEY HAVE TO SWIM TO THE SURFACE TO BREATHE. ONCE THEY HAVE FILLED THEIR LUNGS WITH AIR, THEY WILL RETURN TO THE BELEMNITES.

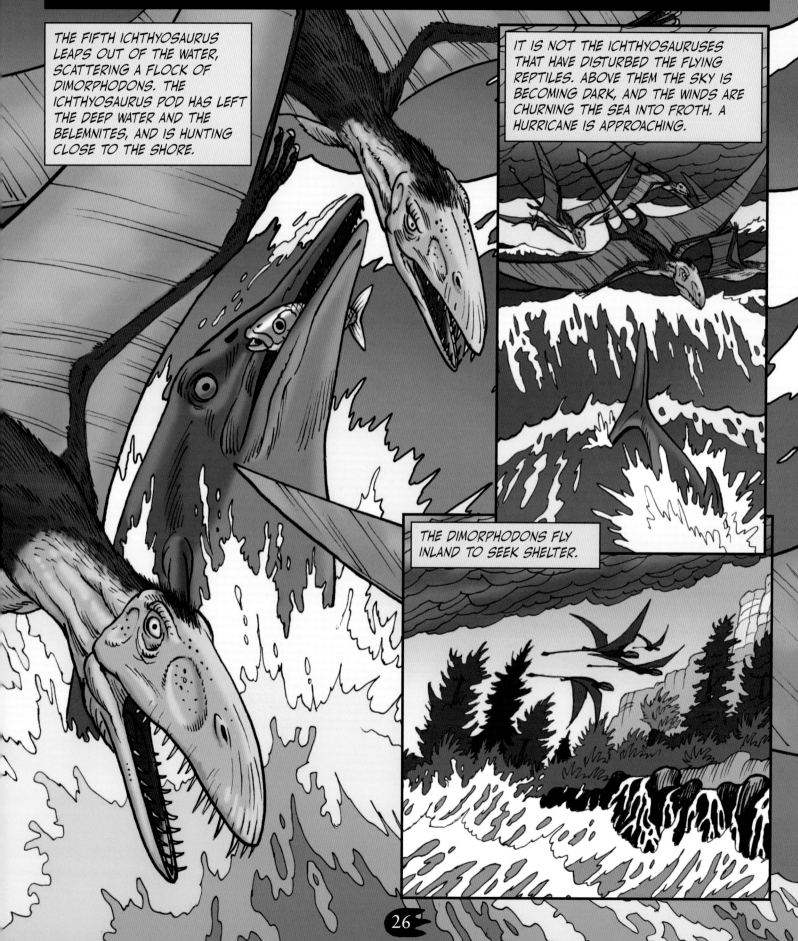

THE FIFTH ICHTHYOSAURUS LEAPS OUT OF THE WATER, SCATTERING A FLOCK OF DIMORPHODONS. THE ICHTHYOSAURUS POD HAS LEFT THE DEEP WATER AND THE BELEMNITES, AND IS HUNTING CLOSE TO THE SHORE.

IT IS NOT THE ICHTHYOSAURUSES THAT HAVE DISTURBED THE FLYING REPTILES. ABOVE THEM THE SKY IS BECOMING DARK, AND THE WINDS ARE CHURNING THE SEA INTO FROTH. A HURRICANE IS APPROACHING.

THE DIMORPHODONS FLY INLAND TO SEEK SHELTER.

THE STORM IS GETTING WORSE BY THE HOUR. A HOWLING WIND RIPS THROUGH THE COASTLINE TREES, WHILE MOUNTAINOUS WAVES CRASH ONTO THE ROCKY SHORE.

THE LARGE WAVES HAVE STIRRED UP THE SAND AND SILT ON THE OCEAN FLOOR. EVEN THE ICHTHYOSAURUSES CANNOT SEE IN THE CLOUDY WATER.

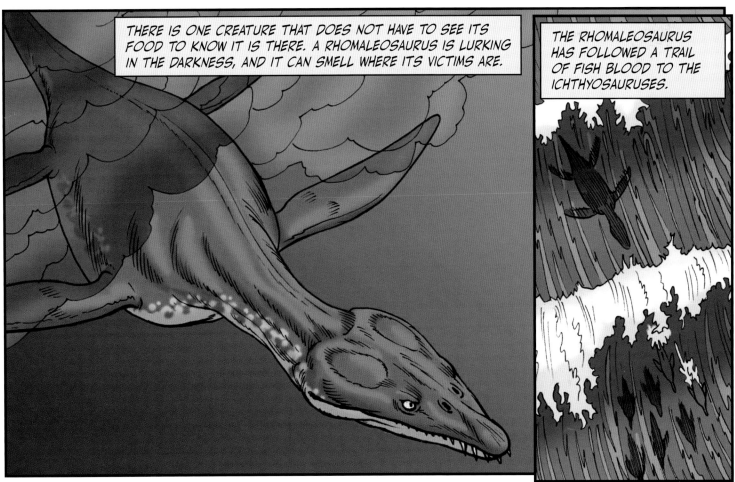

THERE IS ONE CREATURE THAT DOES NOT HAVE TO SEE ITS FOOD TO KNOW IT IS THERE. A RHOMALEOSAURUS IS LURKING IN THE DARKNESS, AND IT CAN SMELL WHERE ITS VICTIMS ARE.

THE RHOMALEOSAURUS HAS FOLLOWED A TRAIL OF FISH BLOOD TO THE ICHTHYOSAURUSES.

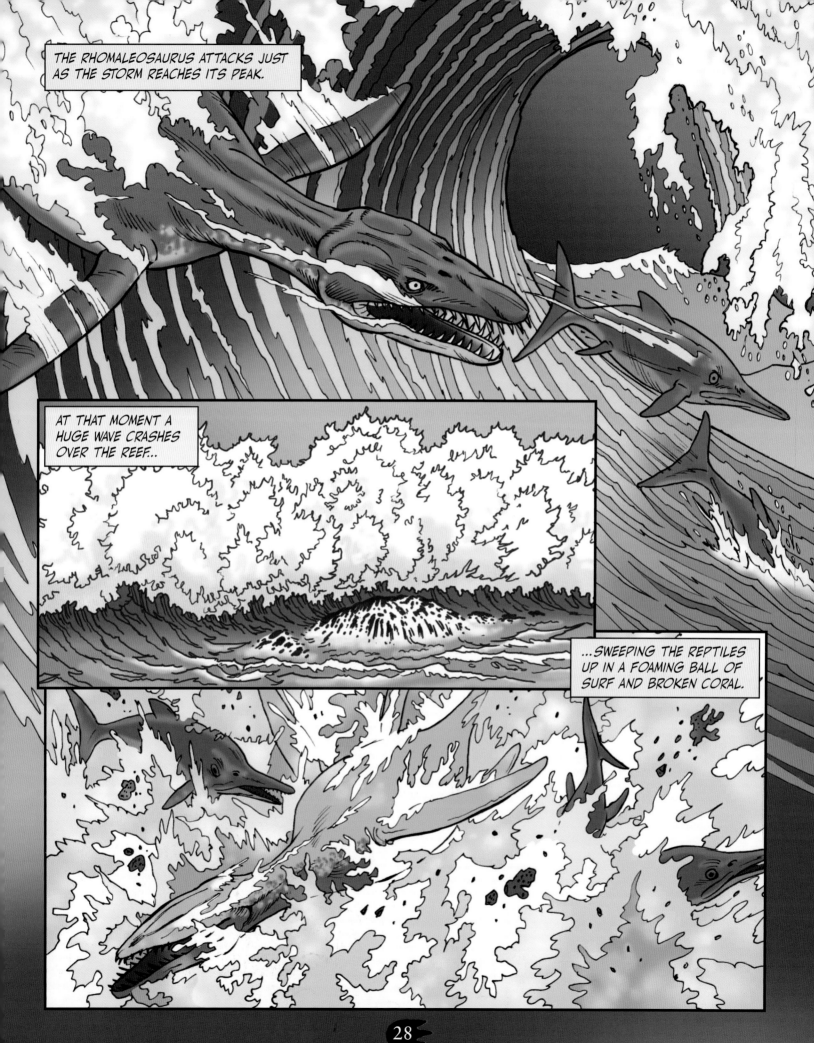

THE RHOMALEOSAURUS ATTACKS JUST AS THE STORM REACHES ITS PEAK.

AT THAT MOMENT A HUGE WAVE CRASHES OVER THE REEF...

...SWEEPING THE REPTILES UP IN A FOAMING BALL OF SURF AND BROKEN CORAL.

THE ICHTHYOSAURUSES FIGHT AGAINST THE RUSHING WAVE. THEIR POWERFUL TAILS AND STREAMLINED SHAPE HELP THEM ESCAPE TO DEEPER AND CALMER WATER.

THE RHOMALEOSAURUS IS NOT SO LUCKY. DESPITE ITS SIZE, THE REPTILE IS LIFTED UP AND THROWN ONTO THE SHORELINE ROCKS.

KERRDOOOM!!!

TIME HAS PASSED, AND THE HURRICANE HAS DIED DOWN. THE ROCKS ARE LITTERED WITH *DEBRIS* FROM THE STORM, INCLUDING THE BODY OF THE RHOMALEOSAURUS. A SARCOSAURUS HAS SEEN IT AND PICKS HIS WAY OVER THE ROCKS TO SCAVENGE ON THE DEAD PLIOSAUR.

FOSSIL EVIDENCE

SCIENTISTS LEARN WHAT DINOSAURS MAY HAVE LOOKED LIKE BY STUDYING THEIR FOSSIL REMAINS. FOSSILS ARE FORMED WHEN THE HARD PARTS OF AN ANIMAL OR PLANT ARE BURIED AND TURN TO ROCK OVER THOUSANDS OF YEARS.

The first complete fossilized Ichthyosaurus skeleton was discovered by Mary Anning and her brother Joseph in Lyme Regis, on the south coast of England in 1811.

This fossil Ichthyosaurus was found in Charmouth, England. It is unusual to find the complete skeleton of a fossilized animal.

At first, scientists thought that ichthyosaurs came onto land to lay their eggs. Then a fossil was found showing a tiny ichthyosaur half inside the body of a larger one. The large animal had not eaten the small one—it had died while giving birth. It proved that ichthyosaurs gave birth underwater to live young.

Some fossilized ichthyosaurs are so detailed that the outline of their body shape can be seen. Scientists know from this that ichthyosaurs had one fin on their backs, as sharks and dolphins do.

The cliffs of Lyme Regis, England (bottom), are famous for their fossils. They are part of a World Heritage Site. Scientists know how big Ichthyosaurus's eyes were by measuring fossils of the bones that protected them (right).

ANIMAL GALLERY

A<small>LL THESE ANIMALS APPEAR IN THE STORY.</small>

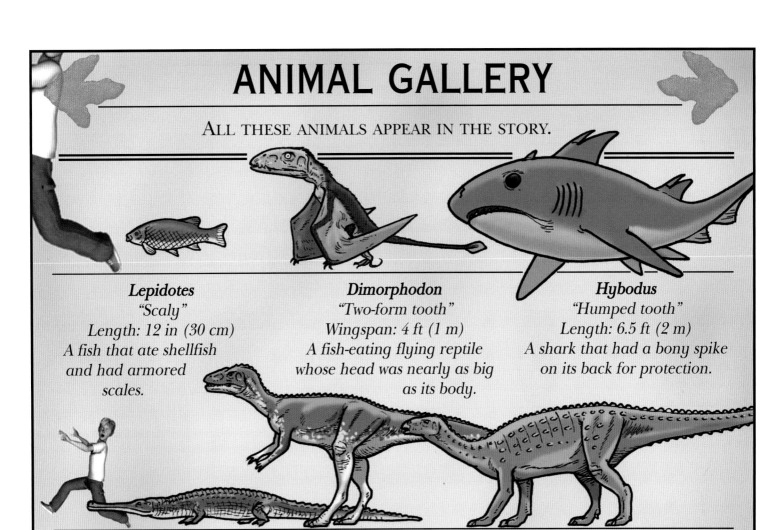

Lepidotes
"Scaly"
Length: 12 in (30 cm)
A fish that ate shellfish
and had armored
scales.

Dimorphodon
"Two-form tooth"
Wingspan: 4 ft (1 m)
A fish-eating flying reptile
whose head was nearly as big
as its body.

Hybodus
"Humped tooth"
Length: 6.5 ft (2 m)
A shark that had a bony spike
on its back for protection.

Teleosaurus
"Complete lizard"
Length: 10 ft (3 m)
A saltwater crocodile that used
its long snout to catch fish.

Sarcosaurus
"Flesh lizard"
Length: 11.5 ft (3.5 m)
A small meat-eating dinosaur.

Scelidosaurus
"Leg lizard"
Length: 13 ft (4 m)
A plant-eating dinosaur that
had rows of bony scales on its
back for
protection.

Plesiosaurus
"Near lizard"
Length: 16 ft (5 m)
A long-necked marine
reptile that ate fish,
belemnites, and
ammonites.

Attenborosaurus
"David Attenborough's
lizard"
Length: 16 ft (5 m)
A meat-eating marine
reptile that had very
large teeth.

Rhomaleosaurus
"Strong lizard"
Length: 23 ft (7 m)
A large meat-eating
marine reptile that
used its good sense of
smell to hunt its prey.

Temnodontosaurus
"Cutting-tooth lizard"
Length: 30 ft (9 m)
A huge ichthyosaur
that could hold its
breath underwater for
20 minutes.

GLOSSARY

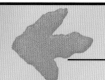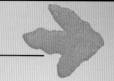

agile (A-jul) Moving quickly and skillfully.

crannies (KRA-neez) Small gaps or openings.

debris (duh-BREE) Broken and scattered material.

digest (dy-JEST) To break down food in the stomach.

fossils (FO-sulz) The remains of living things that have turned to rock.

ichthyosaur (IK-thee-uh-sawr) The name given to the group of Ichthyosaurus-like animals.

Jurassic period (juh-RASS-ik PIR-ee-ud) The time between 208 million and 146 million years ago.

nooks (NUHKS) Sheltered hiding places.

INDEX

Web Sites
Due to the changing nature of Internet links, the Rosen Publishing Group, Inc., has developed an online list of Web sites related to the subject of this book. This site is updated regularly. Please use this link to access the list:
www.powerkidslinks.com/gdino/icth/